Mann
with
Altitude

Jon Wornham

Loaghtan Books
Caardee, Dreemskerry Hill
Maughold
Isle of Man
IM7 1BE

Published by Loaghtan Books

First published: November 2016

Copyright © Jon Wornham 2016

Typesetting and origination by:
Loaghtan Books

Printed and bound by:
Geerings Print Ltd.

Website: www.loaghtanbooks.com

ISBN: 978-1-908060-15-0

Website: www.island-images.uk

To Georgie
for encouragement and support in all things aviation
and so much more

Front cover: Lady Isabella waterwheel, looking south east along the Laxey Valley

Rear cover: Airborne drone on Douglas Head, looking north

Title page: The gooseneck bend on the TT course above Ramsey, looking south west

CONTENTS

Point of Ayre   5

Ramsey   6

Gob-ny-Rona   7

Maughold Head   8

Port Cornaa   9

Laxey   10

Garwick   11

Groudle   12

Onchan   13

Douglas   14

The Braaid   15

Bradda Head   16

Port Grenaugh   18

Langness   19

Castletown   20

Scarlett   21

Port St Mary   22

The Sound   23

Niarbyl   24

Peel   25

St John's   26

Druidale   27

Sulby Glen and Reservoir   28

Snaefell   29

Ballachurry   30

Jurby church   31

INTRODUCTION

For many years I have been interested in how the world looks from above. I think my first experience of such views was when I went on a school holiday to Guernsey from the UK when I was around ten years old. Due to a seamen's strike when we were due to travel we ended up going by air instead of by coach and ferry, and my first experience of flying was in a British Midland Airways Douglas Dakota from Luton. Being unpressurised it flew at a fairly low level and I remember being really impressed with the views of the countryside from the aircraft.

When I left school I went to work in Air Traffic Control and in those days part of the training to be an Air Traffic Controller included a full Private Pilot's Licence which then gave me the opportunity to fly myself around to a certain degree, enjoying the views. Despite letting the licence lapse for a while I regained it in 1997 with the Manx Flyers Aero Club at Ronaldsway. I did quite a lot of flying, mainly around the island, and when the first digital cameras became available from around 2000, usually took one up with me, taking the occasional picture out of the aircraft window, some of which appeared on my Island Images website, which started at around the same time. I finally stopped flying light aircraft in 2003 as it was becoming increasingly expensive and I felt that I was not getting enough flying time in to remain as competent as I wished.

Despite the lack of a pilot's licence I retained an interest in aerial photography and in my final year of work before retiring from Ronaldsway Airport in 2015, became aware of the new trends in radio-controlled multi-rotor helicopters, more commonly known as drones, or officially 'remotely piloted aircraft systems'. Using modern technology such as GPS (global positioning system) and self-stabilising camera gimbals it was apparently possible to shoot quite high quality aerial pictures (and video) without the expense of using a light aircraft.

I bought a DJI Phantom 2 Vision Plus and after a half hour lesson at the vendors, started to teach myself how to use it properly as an aerial camera mount. Apart from just learning how to fly it accurately and, more importantly, safely, the Air Navigation Order contains several specific rules and regulations regarding flying a 'small unmanned aircraft' (legally it is an aircraft just as much as a jumbo jet!) and potential pilots need to study them if they are not going to endanger other users of the air, and persons and property on the ground, and risk prosecution. Guidance on current legislation should be obtained from the UK and Isle of Man Avaiation Authorities.

In very general terms the drone must not be flown more than 400 feet above the launch site and must at all times be kept within visual sight at a maximum of 500 metres away from the operator. It should not be flown closer than fifty metres to a person, vessel, vehicle or structure, or within a congested area of city, town or settlement. During the TT and Manx Grand Prix there are further airspace restrictions published which must be observed. Flying close to an airfield (a rough guide would be closer than three miles) without prior permission of the Air Traffic Control is dangerous and can lead to prosecution of the pilot under the Air Navigation Order.

The aerial imagery used in this book was initially shot with the intention of using it in my Island Images website (www.island-images.uk) although all of the pictures here have been specially selected and processed for the publication. The camera on the Phantom 2 has a very wide-angle lens fitted and this produces quite a bit of distortion towards the edges of pictures. Although this is particularly noticeable where you have a straight horizon like the sea, most of the effects can be remedied by post processing on the computer, albeit resulting in some cropping of the picture edges.

Jon Wornham, July 2016

The Point of Ayre, the most northerly tip of the Isle of Man, just 18 miles south of Burrow Head in Scotland and one of the flattest parts of the island. The hills and mountains of Galloway in Scotland are often visible from here with ferries plying between England and Northern Ireland passing by. Local fishing boats can often be seen passing very close inshore, taking advantage of the sea currents around the point to speed their passage. A vast stony beach, built up into layers by the tides and winds, wraps around the Point, extending for miles down the west and east coasts. There are two lighthouses here, the large one was built in 1818 to a design by Robert Stevenson and stands at just under 100 ft. tall, it was automated in 1991 and the associated keepers' cottages are now privately owned. Due the constantly changing beach area, a smaller lighthouse, known as the

'Winkie' was constructed on the beach in 1899 and was moved in 1950. Use of this smaller light ceased in 2010 and it was recently sold, reputedly for £10,000.

A bustling little port, Ramsey is located on the north east coast and is an important point of entry for cargo boats arriving at the island. The harbour is protected by two long piers but is only usable at high tides as it dries out. There have been proposals to construct a marina here, with water levels protected by a tidal flap-gate, similar to the one in Peel, but so far the harbour remains much as it has been for many years. A swing bridge, usable by both vehicles and pedestrians, was constructed in 1892. On the right is the Ramsey shipyard where the three-masted iron sailing vessel, *Euterpe* was constructed in 1863. Renamed *Star of India* in 1906, she is now preserved at the maritime museum in San Diego, USA.

The only surviving pleasure pier on the island, Queen's Pier, is at Ramsey and although closed is the subject of a rescue bid. It was opened in 1886 and was used to allow passenger steamships to dock at Ramsey in any tidal state, although the berths at the end of the pier were demolished some years ago. A small railway ran along the pier to transport passengers and their luggage. In 1847 Queen Victoria paid a visit to Ramsey on the royal yacht. Although she apparently remained on board suffering from seasickness, Prince Albert ventured ashore and climbed to the top of Lherghy Frissell hill, where a tower was later erected to commemorate the fact.

Close to Ramsey on the east coast is the pretty headland of Gob-ny-Rona, Manx for 'Point of the Seal'. On the northern side of the headland facing Ramsey lies the hamlet of Port Lewaigue whilst on the southern is Port e Vullen. The national coastal path *Raad ny Foillan* or Way of the Gull runs around the headland, but the beach section by Port e Vullen is only usable at low tide. Ramsey can be seen in the distance on the upper picture with the Albert Tower looking down over the town. In the lower picture, Maughold head can be seen to the left rising high above the sea.

When the route of the Manx Electric Railway from Laxey to Ramsey was being planned in the late 1800s, it was at one time proposed to route from where the current line passes Dreemskerry Farm, out to the coast at Port e Vullen and then via Port Lewaigue into Ramsey by the Queen's Pier and along by the harbour to link up with the Manx Northern Railway. For whatever reason, financial or geological, it never happened and the line remained inland, but what a wonderful scenic route it would have been along the coast!

Following the east coast from Gob ny Rona brings us to Maughold Head, rising to around 380 ft. above the sea. It is the closest point of the Isle of Man to England, with St Bees Head being 31 miles to the north east. As such it is a popular route for single engine light aircraft making the Irish Sea crossing. On a clear day the mountains of the English Lake District can be seen from here, often capped with snow during the winter months. Of recent construction, extensive wind turbine farms spread across the horizon in front of the English coast.

Maughold Head is home to another of the island's lighthouses, slightly unusual in that while the associated keepers' cottages are located on the headland at around 150 feet above sea level, the actual lighthouse is located further down the cliffs and reached by a steep pathway. The lighthouse was constructed in 1914, and automated in 1993, with the lighthouse cottages above now a private residence.

At the top of the lower picture the tiny village of Maughold can be seen, with the parish church of St Maughold and its extensive graveyard visible. The present church was built on the site of a Celtic monastery, dating from around 600 AD and the churchyard contains the remains of ancient chapels or keills. The highest point of Maughold head is just behind the lighthouse cottages with the orange Bride Cliffs in the distance behind.

Continuing south along the coast from Maughold brings us to the delightful location of Port Cornaa. Reached by a narrow lane from the Ramsey to Laxey road, a broad shingle beach protects a tidal lagoon, which is alternately filled and drained by the changing tides. The shape of the beach changes from year to year as winter storms and tides batter the stones. There are two cottages here, one tiny one is located on the southern side of the beach with another behind the lagoon.

The Cornaa River can be seen in both pictures. Rising in the steep sided valley to the east of Snaefell, it runs down through the picturesque Ballaglass Glen before entering the sea on the north side of the beach here. There is an excellent walk from Port Cornaa to Ballaglass Glen, mainly through woodland and passing the remains of the Bellite explosives works, construction of which was started in the 1890s by a Swedish company. The intention was to export the finished product from a jetty at Port Cornaa, the two sites being linked by a small railway. The factory was never finished after local objections and motions passed by Tynwald restricting permitted activities. The concrete remains are being slowly reclaimed by nature but provide an interesting sight on the walk.

Continuing our journey south brings us to the pretty village of Laxey built mainly on the slopes of the valley containing the Laxey River. The Manx Electric Railway winds around both sides of the valley on its way from Douglas to Ramsey.

A small harbour was constructed here for exporting metal ores from the Great Laxey Mine, which was located further up the valley. The mine was a major producer of lead and zinc in the 1800s and after initial processing the ore was transported down to the harbour by tramway of 3 ft. gauge. The ore-carrying wagons were run down to the harbour from the washing floors by the power of gravity, presumably being hauled back up by horses. After a fatal accident, horses were attached to the front of trains to regulate speeds on the way down. The Great Laxey Mine is now a major tourist attraction, and part of the 19 in. gauge railway that ran into the mine has been reconstructed together with replica steam locomotives *Ant* and *Bee*.

The outskirts of Laxey can be seen in the top picture of our next location, Garwick, which very appropriately means 'pleasant bay'. In the late 1800s and early 1900s Garwick Glen was a popular tourist spot, with visitors taking the Manx Electric Railway to Garwick station, which even boasted its own stationmaster and refreshment kiosk. Paying sixpence to enter the glen, they could then walk down to the beach, taking refreshments at the inn or tea gardens located by the boating lake in the glen, before continuing onwards to the beach where rowing boats could be hired.

The scenic glen passed into private ownership in the 1960s when it was closed to the public and today the railway station is just a minor halt, the buildings having been demolished in 1979. It is still possible to walk down to the beach, either by a narrow lane from the main road just north of Baldrine or by a footpath from the Clay Head Road. Three of the boathouses on the beach survive and it is still possible for find the 'Smugglers Cave' and 'Hermit's Arch' which were advertised features at the height of tourism.

G roudle is a small inlet on the east coast where the river enters the sea by a small pebble beach. It is home to another of the island's vintage railways, the Groudle Glen Railway. Opened in 1896 it was constructed to 2 ft. gauge as a purely 'pleasure' line to transport passengers arriving on the Manx Electric Railway from the inland terminus at Lhen Coan up to the headland where a Victorian zoo had been constructed housing sea lions and polar bears. The zoo closed at the outbreak of World War Two, but the railway re-opened in 1950 and continued in operation until the 1962 season after which it was abandoned and fell into disrepair.

In the late 1960s/early 1970s some of the land was sold to a commercial company who constructed a small village of holiday cottages on the southern slopes of the valley, which can still be rented today. A group of railway enthusiasts started to restore the railway and in December 1983, after a lot of hard work, the first train ran again from Lhen Coan as far as the headland. Amazingly the two original steam locomotives from the line had survived and the 1896 vintage *Sea Lion* was back in service by 1987. Today the line runs all the way to the old zoo site at Sea Lion Rocks where the remains of the polar bear cages and sea lion pool can still be seen.

Groudle

O nchan village is located just to the north of the island's capital Douglas, indeed viewed from above it is difficult to tell where one ends and the other starts. Originally a small cluster of houses around St Peter's Church, it has expanded over the years in all directions and now has the second largest population after Douglas.

The two pictures give a good idea as to the extent of the village, running from the edge of the sea at Port Jack, inland to Birch Hill by Signpost Corner on the TT course. The large buildings in the top picture are, as the large illuminated sign suggest, the main depot of the Manx Electric Railway which started operations as far as Groudle in 1893 but had reached Laxey by the following year and Ramsey by 1899. Two rows of terraces above follow Royal Avenue East and West on either side of a small glen and part of the Onchan Pleasure Park can be seen to the left.

The lower picture shows the glen and Pleasure Park together with the Port Jack area and the large office building

constructed on the site of the former Douglas Bay Hotel. To its right, an area now used for residential purposes was once the White City amusement park, home of an impressively large roller coaster, amongst other entertainments. It was finally demolished in 1985. The Manx Electric Railway can be seen running alongside the road curving tightly around the office building.

D ouglas is the capital of the Isle of Man and is named after the two rivers that join on its outskirts, the Dhoo and the Glass. It is located on a wide bay and is the major passenger seaport for the island, with ships of the Isle of Man Steam Packet Company plying to the ports of Heysham and Liverpool in England and Belfast and Dublin in Ireland.

On the south side of the bay is Douglas Head with its lighthouse, originally

constructed in 1832 and rebuilt in 1892, being situated at the base of the headland. Predating the lighthouse was a landmark tower on top of the head and now incorporated into the apartments constructed on the site of the former hotel here. During World War Two this was the site of *HMS Valkyrie*, a no doubt very secret training establishment where most of the Royal Navy's radar operators were trained.

Moving inland a few miles from Douglas brings us to The Braaid. One of several ancient sites preserved on the island, The Braaid was a settlement dating back to at least the Iron Age and probably earlier. Of the three structures visible in the picture, the oldest is the round house, a typical Celtic structure of just over 50 ft. in diameter and used as a dwelling house. The walls would have been constructed from stone filled with earth with wooden beams supporting a roof made of brushwood covered with turf. The other structures are from a later date and are longhouses in the Viking style. The two longhouses served different purposes, one would have been used for communal living by several families and the other for housing livestock. The larger, residential, longhouse is around 65 ft long and the other slightly less at around 60 ft. What is interesting about the site as a whole is that it shows the two communities, Celtic and Viking, merging together to form a common society, no doubt with influences from both.

Based on the inland location it was probably a mainly farming community and that is indeed still the main use of land in this area, with traditional fairly small fields bounded by Manx 'hedges', stone walls covered with earth in much the same way as the houses were built. Some of the present day scattered houses of the present day village of Braaid can be seen towards the top left of the picture.

Bradda Head

Bradda Head rises abruptly from the sea to a height of just under 400 ft, topped by an impressive stone tower. The headland protects Port Erin Bay from the north, and a smaller headland to the south makes the bay a sheltered haven. The headland was the location of two mines, the North and South Bradda Mines, and many remains of the mine buildings and shafts can still be seen. Lead and copper were mined here from ancient times up until 1874 when the mines were finally closed. The Milner Tower on the headland was built in 1871 just before the closure of the mines and its viewing gallery can still be accessed via a narrow circular internal stairway. The tower was built in the shape of a key to commemorate William Milner, a prominent safe maker and a local philanthropist.

The pictures were taken at a high tide which hides another historical feature in the bay. Construction of Governor Loch's breakwater commenced in 1863 and a temporary railway was built to aid construction and featuring the first steam locomotive to be seen on the island. Unfortunately, in 1884, a severe storm wrecked the breakwater and only the foundation stones remain, uncovered at low water.

Returning to our journey heading south along the east coast brings us to Port Grenaugh, a large sea inlet. My old Ward Lock 'Red Guide' tells me that it was a 'very popular resort' without giving any further details! Old photographs show a row of holiday chalets at the back of the beach and a café-restaurant. Not far away was the luxurious Arragon Hotel, which is now a private residence located in extensive grounds, although there are several public footpaths leading through some of the grounds and connecting with the coastal footpath.

On the northern headland are the remains of the ancient hill fort Cronk ny Merriu which was an Iron Age promontory fort, later altered to be a Norse coastal lookout position with rectangular building, probably to shelter the watchmen. This site is typical of several around the coast of the island, being situated on a rocky outcrop with the landward side being protected by an earth bank.

Your pilot/photographer can just be seen on the right hand side of the lower picture!

To the w
the land j
forming the area
The whole area,
the small sliver of
the Poyllvaaish bl
formed of limesto
underwater volcar
this limestone from
that helped build
many other build
The quarry is not i
filled with water.
extensive limeston
in the lower picture

The orange tow
now used by local
1940s when a 'Cha
Sea. It occupied mi
up to 360 ft. high ar
and receivers remai

Langness Peninsula is connected to the main part of the island by a narrow isthmus to the south of Ronaldsway Airport. The large bay to the east, Derbyhaven, provides a sheltered anchorage for small boats and to the west is Castletown Bay. The stone tower is known as the Herring Tower and was constructed around the start of the 1800s to act as a landmark for passing shipping. A very narrow circular staircase (with no handrails nowadays!) runs around the inside of the walls allowing access to the top of the tower, probably for use as a lookout or for lighting a beacon to guide ships at night.

The tower was succeeded in 1880 by the lighthouse constructed at Langness Point, with a light that could be seen from near Douglas all the way round to the Calf of Man. It was automated in 1996 and the associated keepers' cottages can now be rented for holidays. There is still a foghorn located here but it has not been used since 1987. The line of six semi-circular constructions date from World War Two, when an RAF gunnery school was located at Ronaldsway. An aircraft would tow a banner behind it and the trainee gunners would attempt to hit it. Each gunner had bullets dipped in a different colour paint so their accuracy could be judged after the banner was dropped on the airfield.

Arguably one of the prettiest drives on the island is the Sulby Glen road, running from the Mountain Road at Bungalow to Sulby village. The top picture is taken from above the lower section looking north. If you look carefully behind the roadside cottage you can make out a steep zig-zagging pathway that climbs the hillside to the abandoned farm, or tholtan, of Killabregga. The hillsides around here have several of these tholtans, a record of past times when hardy families farmed the hillsides using mainly horses as transport and to power machinery.

The second picture shows the Sulby Reservoir, constructed relatively recently in 1982 to provide water supplies for the north of the island. In recent years a pumping system has been installed so that water can be transferred from this reservoir across the hilltops and into the Injebreck Reservoir, which supplies the south of the island.

The final picture is taken from close to the village of Sulby and is looking back along the glen to the north.

An anc
into t
the late 12th o
with many cas
was being use
1891 a new ga

Castletown
narrow street fr
from 1821 to 1

There are se
long breakwate
destrian swing
crosses the
to the middle
and, until recen
quite large
freighters woul
through to pick
gos of scrap m
export. Every y
middle harbour
scene of the Wo
Bath Champi
where contestan
each other pa
in..... tin baths!

At just over 2,000 ft. high, Snaefell is the only place that can be classified as a mountain, although local parlance tends to refer to all of the central peaks as 'the mountains'. The name Snaefell comes from the Norse for 'snow mountain' and indeed in winter times it often has a white cap whilst other parts of the island are snow free. If you don't fancy walking up it's possible to use the Snaefell Mountain Railway from Laxey, constructed in 1895 with the original tramcars still running on it.

The TT motorcycle racecourse uses the main road that runs past Snaefell from Ramsey to Douglas and competitors can reach speeds approaching 200 mph on this section. Unlike the United Kingdom, the Isle of Man has no national upper speed limit, so it is up to motorists and riders to choose a safe maximum speed on this road.

The buildings seen in the lower picture were constructed in the 1950s as the operations block for a radar system that was scheduled to be installed on Snaefell as part of the Cold War 'Rotor' Air Defence system for the UK. Plans changed and it is unlikely the actual radar was ever installed, but the buildings were used for a time as a motorcycle museum, although awaiting a new user now.

Snaefell

 ven a large number of residents seem to be unaware of this Civil War fort in the north of the island and no wonder
as it's not that easy to find in the first place and from ground level can be a little underwhelming! It's only when
you see it from above and in the right lighting conditions that it's full extent can be appreciated. The picture was taken
in February, fairly late on in the afternoon when a low sun angle really accentuates the lines of the fort.

It was constructed in the 1640s on the orders of James, Earl of Derby who had been appointed as Lord of Man
in 1627. When the English Civil War broke out in 1642 he supported the King, Charles I, and the fort was probably
constructed to offer a defence against any invasion by forces loyal to the Parliamentary leader, Oliver
Cromwell. It would seem that the fort was never in fact completed and its location is a bit of a mystery,
well away from the coast in the middle of farmland. There is a possibility that it was intended to be a
hidden 'last retreat' with supplies of food and ammunition for the defenders.

It is a large and imposing structure when seen from above, with thick earth walls protected by four
bastions at the corners, which would allow defenders to fire on anyone attacking the main walls. It was
most likely also surrounded by a moat.

Ballachurry

Jurby was settled by Viking invaders in the 9th century AD who started to convert to Christianity in the following century. The first recorded Christian chapel at Jurby predated this and was likely constructed on the site of an ancient pagan burial ground. The church standing on the site today was completed in 1817.

In 1937 the RAF commenced construction of a major training airfield in Jurby to train navigators and gunners and at one time had around 100 aircraft based at Jurby airfield. The flying training activities however took their toll of lives and there is a special area of the churchyard dedicated to military gravestones which can be seen on the right hand side of the upper picture.

The airfield is still there and can be seen in the background of the lower photograph, however there is little aviation activity now and the airfield is used more for motorsports, mainly motorcycle racing. The old technical site for the airfield is a thriving industrial business park and also houses two museums, the Isle of Man Motor Museum, opened in 2015, and the Transport Museum, located just across the road. The new Isle of Man prison is also located on part of the old airfield site, opening in 2008.

Jurby church

ACKNOWLEDGEMENTS

DJI for manufacturing a very user friendly range of consumer drones with many safety features built in.

Ronaldsway Air Traffic Services, management and operational controllers & assistants for helpful co-ordination when flying in the vicinity of Ronaldsway Airport and useful discussions on the legal aspects of drone flying under Isle of Man legislation.

UK National Air Traffic Services for very useful advice on amateur vs commercial use of a drone.

The Isle of Man Aviation Authority for guidance notes on flying a 'drone' in Isle of Man airspace.

HeliGuy.com for some very useful advice even though I didn't buy the drone from them – but probably next time!

All of the people who have posted very informative drone videos on YouTube.

SELECTED BIBLIOGRAPHY

An Illustrated Encyclopedia of the Isle of Man, David T. Webber, revised Frank Cowin and F.J.Radcliffe, The Manx Experience, 1977

Chronicles of Man, *vol 1-3*, various, Lily Publications, undated

Scottish and Manx Lighthouses, Ian Cowe, The Northern Lighthouse Heritage Trust, 2015

Things to do with Vikings, Sara Goodwins, Loaghtan Books, 2014

Journey on the Manx Electric Railway, Chris Pulling, Train Crazy Publishing, 2015

The many contributors to Wikipedia articles on the Isle of Man

Whitestrand, looking north